CW00538304

# Agile Coaching as a Success Factor

## Basics of coaching to successfully manage Agile teams

**by Markus Heimrath**

# Table of Contents

# 1. What Is Agile and What Is Agile Coaching?

If you wanted to introduce new methods or processes in a company in the past (and still do in some cases today), you would hire consulting firms that spent a year working on how best to implement the project and then formulating a project plan with milestones and goals.

Today, there is often no time for long preliminary planning. Methods and processes are needed where changes can still be made while the project is running. Today, the business environment has become so uncertain that you can hardly plan more than six months in advance.

One of the methods where less planning is done in advance and more is done right from the start is the Agile Framework. Essentially, it is a method by which requirements and solutions for products are created during an ongoing process that is characterized by teamwork, self-organization, and the needs of the end user or customer. Agile methods had their origin in software development and are now the standard when it comes to developing new software products. But they can, with small modifications, also be applied in other business areas.

To run a project in an agile environment—for example, to develop software—you don't even need much prior knowledge. The manifesto on which the Agile Principle is based can be viewed by everyone, and the most important steps can already be read at Wikipedia today. Nevertheless, the best theory is not enough if you suddenly face reality. This is where the Agile Coach comes in.

Coaching at Agile is a bit like the job of a manager in a football team. The players actually all know what they have to do; there is a coach who determines the training sessions and makes them fit. The manager takes care of the strategy and ensures that they have the right environment.

At Agile, the coach is the person who lays the foundation for working successfully with an agile framework. A coach creates the prerequisites for being able to introduce agile methods at all. If, for example, you consider introducing Scrum to develop software, it will be the coach's job to advise and support the company but above all to ensure that everyone has the same understanding of the project.

# 2. The Difference between a Scrum Master and an Agile Coach

Since Scrum is the best known Agile method, it is often asked what the difference is between a coach and the Scrum Master. If you want to become a coach, you will already know what the Scrum Master basically does. There are some fundamental differences between the two roles but also similarities.

The Scrum Master and the agile Coach both take care of the same problem, namely to lead an agile project to success, but on different levels. The coach usually has a somewhat broader task, not only taking care of the team, but also the higher management and other stakeholders and above all other teams. He is understood as the expert who can answer all questions (which is not the case in practice), who can not only lead discussions, but also analyse them. He gives feedback and can show the way to go:

- What has to be done?
- What training does the team-leader need?
- Who needs further training?

- What do you do with a team that works too slowly?

There are also differences in payment. Because the tasks of the coach are broader, he is also better paid than a Scrum Master, who only has to take care of one team. Ultimately, it also depends on the industry you work in and the size of the company that hired you. Young companies in particular often try to save on coaching because they see no immediate benefit, while large companies understand the long-term effect and are willing to invest in it.

The biggest difference, however, is what is expected of you. Usually the Scrum Master works with a single team, while the coach has to advise several teams and stakeholders. The Scrum Master must above all ensure that the Scrum process is adhered to, that there are stand-up meetings, that the product backlog is conducted properly and that the sprints are completed. The coach, on the other hand, must determine what needs to be done at all, how it can be done, who does it, when it is done and how this is possible within the existing structures. His tasks can even include change management, leadership training and workshops. He is often also a mediator between different departments and teams within an organization.

| Scrum Master | Agile Coach |
| --- | --- |
| • Leads a project<br>• Has a defined function<br>• Is team committed | • Can train multiple teams<br>• Is free in his coaching<br>• Supports the Scrum Master |

# 3. Requirements for a coach

You don't become a coach overnight or even if you have attended one or two seminars. It is above all an understanding of what you do and how you understand yourself. It is also a question of character: if you are a very reserved person who doesn't like to approach people, you will have difficulties in the beginning. If you're quick-tempered, you can't build a trusting relationship with the team. The same is true for self-opinionated people. It doesn't matter what technique you use in coaching if you don't have the necessary human skills.

**Empathy**

The ability to understand the other person and to understand in front of everyone what he feels and what drives him is one of the most important qualities that a coach must bring with him. Most problems within teams - but also between different hierarchical levels - are interpersonal. Only when you are able to understand not only the technical and organizational structures, but also the people you are dealing with, will you be able to connect with them.

## Overview

A good coach shouldn't be around little things. You are not a project manager, but you have to keep track and be able to look at problems from a different point of view. However, you still need to know what is going on in the team itself and what problems arise there. At the same time, however, you will have to consider the interests of the entire company and its management.

## Motivation

A team can only be motivated by a coach if it respects him and feels connected to him. Your main task will be to earn your respect, and that means more than just having expertise. If the team you are working with is convinced that you know what you are talking about and that you are able to implement it successfully, you have already laid the foundation for a good project.

In addition, there are some other requirements for a good coach. He should be expected to make a team more effective by having **ideas put forward and discussed by everyone within the team**, but at the same time such discussions are goal-oriented and improve the workflow rather than stop him.

Furthermore, a coach should ensure that the **team** is not just made up of individual experts, but **is as diverse as possible** - this also includes members who, for example, do not have a programming background. At the same time, as a coach you will need to be able to solve the problems that diversity can cause.

**When a coach asks a question, it should always be an open question that leads the team to look for a solution instead of just answering yes or no. A good coach does not solve the team's problems, but helps the members to solve them themselves.**

In many cases this means that you have to **take a step back** and wait and see how the team solves the problem - even if you already have a good solution in mind. Part of a coach's job is to build capacity in a company. This also includes the ability of a coach to make it clear to the trainee what responsibilities they have and that they are also responsible for their work to other employees instead of just a department manager or project manager.

Finally, as a coach you will also have to stand in front of your team when conflicts arise within a company or organisation. This is not easy if you are brought in from outside, and sometimes even more difficult if you coach within your company. But in the event of a case, standing up for the team will earn you not only the respect of the team itself, but also of those against whom you defend the team. Of course this always depends on who is on the other side, in some cases you will run against walls, but that is not your responsibility. It is important that you give your best.

When a coach is hired, there are two ways to judge him, pay him and define his work:

- **qualitative results and**

- **quantitative results**

The **quantitative results** concern everything that can be expressed in numbers:

- How many people are being coached?

- How many hours are being charged/used?

- By what percentage should output improve?

- How much money do you want to save through improvement?

- How much fever errors occurred?

- How fast are Products being tested?

- How quickly are products ready for delivery?

- How has the burndown chart improved?

Such numbers are quite easy to get, but they don't say much about how successful a coach really was. That's why there will always be qualitative results that you can write down as a goal when you start coaching. Such results can be:

- Employees are able to solve problems quickly and efficiently within the team

- There is a common understanding of backlog items

- Employees also get tasks that present a challenge for them

- Team members are able to coach the next project independently

Other qualitative results may also be of a technical nature, such as that the Clean Code practice has been adapted and a new programming language has been successfully introduced.

# work samples

Chandan Lal Patary, himself a coach and speaker at many Agile conferences, presented in his LinkedIn-Feed some work examples that companies give candidates for a coaching job.[1]

*Power Auto was under enormous pressure to succeed. Its products were already a box office hit in Europe and the company wanted to take over the American market quickly. But with the previous products this was hardly possible, the maintenance costs were too high. The existing customer base was large, but the existing technology was outdated and could not be expanded. Customers, on the other hand, were always demanding new functions. The company had a development center in Germany with 35 employees and a test team in India with 20 employees. The product itself was over 20 years old, most of the employees who developed it had long since retired.*

*The management had decided to develop a new product similar to the previous one, but equipped with the latest technology. The time frame for the development was*

---

[1] Lal Patary, C. (2017): Case Studies on Agile Transformation. URL: https://www.linkedin.com/pulse/case-studies-agile-transformation-chandan-lal-patary/ [Date of Reference: 08--08-2018]

*estimated at 2-3 years. The market demands a fast product with current features and a short feedback cycle. Some of the employees in the company have been with the company for over 20 years. Few employees are familiar with the latest technologies. 50 percent of the budget is spent on maintaining the existing product (troubleshooting/customer inquiries). Investments in new developments are a challenge. The company has decided to tackle these challenges with an agile transformation project. The challenges:*

- *How can we move faster to new technology and reach new markets?*

- *What should be the strategy of the company to cope with such a situation?*

- *What technology migration and upgrades are required?*

- *How do you communicate this to existing customers?*

- *The competitor already has a new modern product on the market:*
  *How can you help the team as an Agile Coach? What are the first steps you would take? What is your plan and model?*

# 4. Who's being coached?

The tasks of an agile coach depend strongly on who is to be coached at all. Of course, it makes a difference if you only have to train a small software team or if you have to use agile methods in all processes of a global company.

The three main coaching groups are:

- **Organizations and companies as well as management levels**
- **Coaching of teams in software development and project management**
- **Coaching to introduce Agile as a concrete framework**

To illustrate how important it is that not only individual teams but also entire companies are trained to take problems seriously and solve them at the same time instead of ignoring them, the <u>catastrophe of the US space shuttle Challenger</u> is a good example.

The shuttle was ready to go, the day was clear and cold, colder than previous starts. One of the engineers of a supplier company for NASA had warned that the cold could be a risk. They had never tested certain gaskets at the temperatures they were at, and he was afraid that there might be a malfunction. He also raised these concerns in a video conference with NASA - and was asked to reconsider his warning to abort the launch. NASA's pressure on the small subcontractor was so great that they actually gave in - with the result that all crew members died. The underlying problem was that they wanted to move forward with the plan instead of improving the product on the spot or stopping production in this case the launch—until the problem was solved.

If you now know what you actually want to achieve, you can think about which different techniques and methods you want to use and which, above all, suit the team or organisation best. This is an important step that sometimes goes astray when certain wishes have already been expressed, such as introducing Scrum or eXtreme Programming. This may be a wish of the management, but it doesn't always have to be the best solution for the problem, the previous way of working or the team itself. The well-known Agile Coach Alan S. Koch has published some thoughts[2] on this subject. When it comes to reorganizing an organization and minimizing workload, Scrum, for example, makes little sense and project management such as Kanban Boards is much more appropriate.

 **What to look out for:**

- The culture of a company and a department

- How customers (want to) cooperate with the company

- What projects are there?

- Which tools and processes are already in use?

- The strengths and weaknesses of the development team in particular

- How the company is structured

At Agile, it's always about ensuring that teams can work as independently as possible. The developers are not told

---

[2] Koch, A. S.: Adopting an Agile Method (2006). URL: http://www.methodsandtools.com/archive/archive.php?id=41 [Date of Reference: 16-08-2018]

what to do and what not to do and when to do something. They just get a formulation of the goal they want to achieve and can then work with the client to find ways to achieve that goal. As a coach you must not forget that it is autonomy that you want to promote.

If you work in a company where much is decided from above, then Agile will be a challenge for you. But it won't be easy for the company itself and its management to change a **certain management style** just like that. The management in particular will have to learn to let go and to give up responsibility and control.

 **Those who have been department heads for years will initially find it difficult to work in a team that they are not allowed to instruct.**

An Agile Coach must recognize this problem in time and possibly hold workshops that bring all participants to the same denominator when it comes to understanding Agile. What you want to avoid is a team that is ready to work with Scrum and has a product manager in the room every day who gives instructions.

The same applies to the **planning departments** in many companies. A widespread practice, which has worked for decades, has been to make a plan and then execute it. At the end of the project, you saw the result and any problems were written into the final report, which was then filed somewhere. The Agile Coach is the natural enemy of all planners because you will have to convince them that many things cannot be planned at all. That's why Agile's planning is very abstract and formulates goals rather than ways. In the course of the project, adjustments are made. Such planning thinking is firmly anchored, and you will have to consider how you can change that thinking.

**Planning and definitions in particular can become a problem**. If the company you work for expects you to present plans and milestones to management, or such plans and milestones have priority and are pillars of the project, then you won't get far with Agile methods, no matter how well you can coach a team. Agile is the knowledge of not knowing, expecting the unexpected, and not planning. Especially when coaching management levels it will be your main task to anchor a shift from planning to agility in your mind.

# 4.1 Coaching of Organizations

If a company hires you as an Agile Coach, then your main task will be to provide a basic understanding of Agile methods and to create the necessary capacity to use Agile processes at all. In this job you will have to do a lot of convincing. A classic example is a medium-sized company that has so far implemented software for customers in the banking industry with classic waterfall project management. There is a good chance that you will meet more conservative managers who also have conservative customers, namely bankers. For them, security always comes first, and change often means a threat to security, even if it is objectively unfounded. Here it will be less the task to explain which task a Scrum Master has than to fundamentally to take away the fears and to introduce the executives slowly to the topic.

## 4.2 Coaching of Teams

The main task of an Agile Coach in medium and large companies is to coach the different teams that have either started to work with Agile methods or are already doing so. Your task here is not to intervene in the respective project but above all to support the team leaders—for example, the Scrum Masters—in their work and to help them solve problems. In practice it can look like this:

A company that creates accounting software tailored to the client has several development teams worldwide. These teams work in different time zones but also have different work attitudes, often cultural, or different perceptions of priorities. This can lead to delays when one team has to deliver products to another team. Even if a team works very well with Scrum, for example, it can still happen that there are problems within an organization because working methods are not sufficiently harmonized.

Your job as a coach will then be to bring the different team leaders together and help them to better align the Agile processes with each other.

What a team coach usually works on:

- Responsibilities within autonomous teams

- Support in the implementation of measures

- Helping the team make better decisions and resolve conflicts

- Creating transparency

- Identifying hurdles and barriers

- Improving relationships between the Product Owner and the team

- Explaining the principle of ownership

- Improving Scrum techniques

- Preparing the Scrum Master for its task

Often you will work like a Scrum Master in team coaching. Especially at the beginning, the Scrum Master or other roles can work with you until they are able to fulfill their role alone.

## Typical Tasks

### Perform Scrum Meetings

Teams can always improve, especially when it comes to sprint planning, and your task is to help them. The same applies to other Scrum elements such as Retrospective, Daily Scrum and Backlog Refinement. You can offer workshops before the start of the project in which these techniques will be trained. The same applies to other methods like Kanban: Here you can prepare the team on how to formulate a practicable definition of Done and how to subdivide the boards best. But always remember that you should only give suggestions. The team should solve the problem itself.

### Creating a Common Basis

Particularly when teams are newly assembled, there are different ideas about how the work can be done. Questions can arise like "Can a developer also test?" or "How long can work be parked at Kanban?" but also who takes over the work if someone fails or how the team then distributes the work. Workshops in which you can play through different scenarios and help the team to define its own working methods will also help here.

**The Shadow of the Scrum Masters**

What sounds a little threatening is meant positively. You will take over many of the tasks of the Scrum Masters, especially when coaching a team at the beginning. Your task, however, is to hand them over as soon as possible. However, so that the team leader is not simply thrown into the cold water, you should help him or her. You don't monitor or control and you don't give instructions. Your job is to help when the Scrum Master no longer knows what to do. You can also have feedback sessions if you wish.

**Observing the Team**: The more problems you observe at the beginning, the easier it will be for the team to work together. That's why you look over the team's shoulder without giving directives. As a coach, you will want to know above all how communication takes place, whether there are misunderstandings and how these can be eliminated. Sometimes these misunderstandings can arise simply by using different terms, for example English and German terms.

**Team Discussions:** The best way to find out how the team feels is to have very casual feedback sessions that don't take long and can be easily done in between.

# 4.3 Coaching to Introduce an Agile Framework

Whenever a team changes its way of working from classical project management to an agile method such as Scrum or Kanban, a coach is usually brought on board to support and advise in this process. Your task here is less to introduce Scrum yourself than to help the project manager and the Scrum Master to make the team fit for Agile methods. Let's assume that a software company wants to become more efficient but doesn't want to change their complete way of working. You take a new assignment as an opportunity to first let a team work with Scrum. You have already trained a Product Owner and a Scrum Master. Now it's a matter of offering support to all participants and enabling them to recognize and solve emerging difficulties themselves. This role is often confused with the role of the Scrum Master, but the two roles differ. An essential difference is that you are also the coach of the Scrum Master.

When it comes to technically implementing an Agile method, your expertise and experience with projects will be in great demand. This is where it pays off if you have previously held roles in Scrum or other techniques. Your task is to improve technical skills. Such can be:

How to write better code: Each team develops certain peculiarities that sometimes have to be changed

- Explain Clean Coding practices and introduce them to the team

- Help the team to convert the existing code into a clean and structured code

- Formulate test scenarios

- To help facilitate more and more intensive testing to introduce a test driven environment

- Automate tests

- Introducing new working methods

Very often you will also sit together with a team member and you will work together on code (pair coding). This is a very efficient method because it is an intensive training and at the same time real work is done. However, you will have to be self-disciplined so that you don't spend all your time sitting next to developers. Especially if you are a programmer yourself, this can sometimes be tempting.

Here are the tasks of an Agile Coach for an introduction to methods like Scrum at a glance:

- **Accompany Scrum Events**. Teams often have a lot of improvement potential in Sprint Planning, Daily Scrum, Review and Retrospective and Backlog Refinement. A coach can first play through such processes with workshops and try them out on various models.

- **Training Courses and Workshops** for the joint creation of work rules. A good understanding of Scrum and self-governing teams is necessary before a team begins its journey as such a self-governing team.

- **Looking Over Your Shoulders**. A team coach is often a temporary Scrum Master. But after a while he usually hands over the Scrum Master job to someone else. He spends a lot of time explaining things to the Scrum Master and coaching him by looking over his shoulder and giving feedback.

- **Observation** and **One-To-One Discussion**. A team coach will spend a lot of time simply observing how the team and its environment work, looking for improvement opportunities, giving feedback and asking questions that help the team reflect.

- **Discussions** with team members about the team structure and collaboration, Scrum and practices of appreciation within the team.

# 5. Basics of Agile Coaching

Before you learn which steps you will take as an Agile Coach, you should know some of the basics of Agile coaching. One of them is that you should be familiar with the essential Agile frameworks, at least Scrum and Kanban. It's ideal if you've done projects with Scrum or similar yourself before or at least were part of such a team. Most of the time you will have a much better understanding of what goes on in such a project. If you don't have any knowledge in this respect yet, then you are strongly advised to read up on it or attend a corresponding workshop.

## 5.1 Why Teamwork Is More Important Than the Coach

In **sports**, the coach's main task is to set up a team that delivers excellent results—winning games and becoming a champion. On the one hand, this means that the coach has to know a lot about his sport, which is why many successful coaches are also former top athletes. They usually work on improving the skills of the individual players, positioning the team tactically and motivating them accordingly. But this is not possible without the cooperation of the team. In football, a coach is usually dismissed when he is no longer able to develop the team further, motivate it or put it on the right tactical footing.

As an **Agile Coach** you face similar but not the same tasks: You will have to see who is best in the team in which area and how these people can be deployed and motivated. But you don't want a star striker who has to get the balls from the others. In software development, the most important thing is that the team can work together. You have to help him collaborate and organize the work so that it runs smoothly and evenly. You will have to identify bottlenecks and eliminate them together with the team.

The **big difference to a football coach** is that you don't give instructions. You don't stand on the edge and wave your arms and scream at the goalkeeper. Instead, you make sure that everyone can do their job. This may be less emotional, but you also need to keep your team going longer than 90 minutes.

# 5.2 What Significance Does the Agile Manifesto Have for Coaching?

The basis of Agile software development, but also of all other Agile techniques, is presented in the Agile manifesto, in which the most important basic rules are laid down. It is something like the basic law of the Agile movement, and as a coach you should not only know it but also internalize it.

**Manifesto for Agile Software Development**

"We open up better ways to develop software by doing it ourselves and helping others do it.

Through this activity, we have learned to appreciate these values:

- Individuals and interactions more than processes and tools

- Functioning software more than comprehensive documentation

- Cooperation with the customer more than contract negotiation

- Responding to change more than following a plan

This means that although we find the values on the right important, we rate the values on the left higher."[3]

For you as an Agile Coach this means that your focus is more and more on the people involved and not on adhering to **organizational or functional rules**. It also means that you need to develop a functioning product and steer your team in that direction. **Cooperation** is also understood to the extent that the customer and the end user are involved as early and as far as possible, and not just at the time the contract is signed and the software is delivered. After all, **flexibility** is the most important element in an Agile project:

You will always have to be able to change something, a process, team members, the scope, the sequence, the schedule. Particularly if you train several teams or organizations, this will be one of the most difficult points because the bigger and more experienced an organization is, the more it sticks to its plans.

---

[3] Agilemanifesto.org: Manifesto for Agile Software Development. URL: http://agilemanifesto.org/ [Date of Reference: 14-07-2018]

# 6. The Three Steps of Agile Coaching

Just as every coach in sport has developed his own methods over time, you as a coach will have your own tips and tricks. But there are at least three steps or phases that every coach goes through and which are the same in almost all projects. The only difference is the length of the phases, which usually depends on how well you already know a company and the team.

## 6.1 Assessing the Situation

Before you even meet a team for the first time, you should first check where you are. If you are hired as an external consultant by a company, you should first walk through the building and get a feel for how work is done here. Do the employees sit together a lot, are there many team areas or just a handful of conference rooms, are partitions used in the open-plan office or do the employees share tables and work areas? Is there a coffee kitchen and other rooms or areas where you can distract yourself or rest for a moment?

When you meet the team for the first time, it is important that you find your place at these meetings.

 ***Are you sitting at the top of the table or in the middle or on one of the side chairs?***

*You should refrain from taking the lead because this could send a false signal to the team. A round table is best; if it doesn't exist, sit on one of the long sides.*

After briefly introducing yourself to the team (especially your resume and what else you do), you can roughly outline what your job here is. Don't go into too much detail because you first want to know what the employees need and want.

In some projects you will also talk to the management first or the project management or, for example, only with the Scrum Master. But the procedure is always the same:

 **Try to find out where there can be problems and how you can help.**

It is not always easy for managers to admit that they need help. However, the fact that you have been called shows that you are at least basically willing to accept help. You will also experience that you simply get the coach because you don't have your own capacities and want to get a Scrum project up and running as quickly as possible. In larger organizations it can happen that you have to replace another coach because you are not satisfied with him or her.

If teams are already working with Agile methods, you should first spend some time observing how this is done. Ask questions to understand how to work, but avoid making suggestions on how to improve or criticize.

 **Your job here is to understand and experience as much as possible.**

It will happen again and again that a team or executives first show resistance, and this can be for different reasons: They are afraid of change, they have not been asked before, or they are simply too busy and don't really have time. There are many ways to reduce such resistance. The company itself can involve the employees in the project even before it hires you. Your imagination and introduction can also be decisive: If you are described as an external expert who is supposed to put things in order, it can be counterproductive. It's better to present you as a helper who should show a new perspective on things. In some companies it can also be helpful if you refer to previous projects and how you worked there.

**But you should not exaggerate and show off with your successes.**

After this exploration phase, you will set to work to determine the exact scope of your work. The more closely you have observed, the better you will be able to formulate this catalogue of requirements. It goes far beyond the briefing you have received from the company. As a rule, such a preliminary report is also required by your clients before you receive the entire assignment. You will probably discover a lot of problems and things that can be improved. However, you should only focus on those areas where coaching can help. If a Scrum Meeting takes place in the evening instead of in the morning, it makes little sense but does not fall within your area of responsibility. It is interesting for you why this was done and who suggested (or ordered) it.

Try to make a list of the tasks that you feel are most urgent and that you think coaching can help with. Such a list can include:

- Team building

- General Scrum training

- Introduction to Agile

- Communicate external views

- Workshops

- How to plan sprints better

- Creating balance between stakeholders

- How to collaborate

- Teams without a chef

This list should only give you a few ideas about what can take priority. You'll probably be most likely to see where there is room for improvement based on company observations and employee interviews. By the way, a coach is not only called in to solve problems. He can also help to simply continue or improve an already functioning and successful team.

## 6.1.1 Find Champions

It will be a real help if you can find champions within the team. This means those employees who quickly understand what you are explaining and are able to communicate it to others. They are your allies and many things will be easier for you if you have champions as helpers.

A German software developer, Karsten Aichholz, has had this experience in a multicultural environment. He ran a software company in Thailand, and that meant many language problems, even if the company language was English. There were also differences in how certain things were understood. His method was to first explain to the whole team what to do and then rely on his champions to explain what they said to the team members. In doing so, he ensured that everyone was taught together and that he not only spoke to department heads as in a hierarchical structure but also that the information really reached everyone and was understood. If there were any questions, they could be asked by the champions as well as by the employees.

As an Agile Coach you will be happy to have such translators at your side, even if it's not about language and cultural problems.

## 6.1.2 Find a Mentor

When you are working as an Agile Coach for the first time, it can be useful to get a mentor to help you reflect. This person does not have to be present at the project itself but can sit down with you once or twice a week to talk about the coaching work so far. A mentor should be an experienced Agile Coach who has also carried out or at least worked on Agile projects. His task is to coach the coach, to give you support and above all courage and to listen to you. At the very beginning you will be happy when you can talk to someone about your first steps as a coach and about difficulties that have arisen as well as about the first successes that you have experienced.

## 6.1.3 Listening Needs to Be Learned

A good coach is a good listener. You will be able to advance your team especially well if you listen to it. But listening has to be learned. As a professional you know a lot better. Rachel Davies and Liz Sedley in their standard work Agile Coaching[4] give tips on how to become a good listener and which signals you can send out so that your counterpart also knows that you are listening:

---

[4] Davies R. / Sedley, L. (2009): Agile Coaching

- Create space and space: Don't just go to meetings and talk about yourself. If there are pauses in conversations, you don't necessarily have to fill them.

- Be open: Have a relaxed and open facial expression, do not seem tense and as though you're concentrating too hard. Otherwise, the team might think you are judging it.

- Show interest: Use your eyes, look others in the face, and keep making eye contact with team members without staring at them. In this way you can show that you are really with them.

- Confirm: Nod if you have understood something or give other feedback, like a "Yes," "Hm," or something similar.

# 7. Active Coaching

After you have analyzed all the observations and compiled a list of the most important points, the day comes when you first get together with the team to work. If the introduction was still a formal matter, it is now a matter of finding the right tone, attitude and sometimes behavior. A lot of what a coach does happens subconsciously, and it is only positive if you know some tricks that are helpful in coaching.

Sabrina Spiegel and Stefan Zumbrägel[5] have described how this happens in practice and what challenges you will face:

> "Working together with the client, we have noticed that the teams have found it difficult to formulate a sprint goal. The result was goals like 'all items have to be finished' or 'content XY is being worked on'. The problem with these goals was that nobody noticed them anymore. The focus on features to be created also caused problems in the Sprint Review when

---

[5] Spiegel, S. / Zumbrägel, S.: Coaching Tipps: Hier finden Sie hilfreiche Tipps für den Alltag von Scrum Mastern, Agile Coaches und Agile Leader - Von der Wirkung aus gedacht. URL: https://www.it-agile.de/wissen/coachingtipps/ [Date of Reference: 20-07-2018]

*presenting the Sprint results. In order to counter this problem, we made use of one point from the area of User Story Mapping: think in terms of effect. How does this change the sprint target?*

*When searching for a sprint target, we and the team asked ourselves the question: What does the development in this sprint change noticeably or visibly for the user? And perhaps even more important: What added value does he get if, for example, we worked on the product for 2 weeks?*

*This had various positive effects on the work in the team:*

- *in every sprint an MVP, Minimal Viable Product, was created, and with it the*
- *possibility to get feedback*
- *flexibility in feature design during sprints*
- *better feedback in the review*
- *a much stronger focus on the user*

*It is also exciting that we were able to apply this thinking to the planning of releases."*

# 7.1 Why One Does Not Have an Answer to Everything

Your job as a trainer and coach is not to impart knowledge. Team members can get this from other sources. So if you want to know which test procedures are the best, you can read about it for yourself. But when it comes to finding out which testing procedures are best for the current project, you can help the team set criteria and create a selection process. The team members know best what needs to be tested, how it needs to be tested, and how it should work. In Agile Coaching you always wear two hats: On the one hand you are a coach and facilitator, on the other hand you are a teacher and mentor for the team. With the first hat you try to set processes in motion or to oversee them. This means, for example, that it is your job to call a meeting and perhaps set up an agenda in consultation, but it is not your job to discuss the content. As a teacher and mentor, on the other hand, you can contribute your expertise, for example by explaining how a similar problem was solved in another company or by explaining alternative ways to go about it (for example, when it comes to different programming languages or explaining what Clean Code practice is).

**You will have to tell your team that you are not the Internet or Wikipedia.**

Your task is not to have an answer to everything but to enable others to find the answer. And this also means that there can be situations that can overwhelm even a coach—for example, when certain team members simply do not want to follow certain rules. In this case, there is no blanket solution, and you will have to consider options from a staff meeting to termination.

# 7.2 Selling Changes

One of the most difficult tasks as an Agile Coach, especially when it comes to introducing Agile methods in organizations and larger teams, is selling change. Because even if it was decided from the very top that an Agile method should be used now, this does not mean that it will be celebrated with fireworks. Your task is therefore also to take out tensions. One approach for you is to "sell" the changes. You will have to devise a marketing strategy in order not only to convince the employees but also to inspire them. As with all changes and purchases, the focus is on one specific question: What do I get out of it? You will have to find answers to this question, but to make life a little easier for you, here is a selection of arguments that speak in favor of switching to an Agile method:

**More personal responsibility:** Even if there are always employees who only want to carry work out, this argument will inspire those who are tired of just following orders.

**Real teamwork:** In a team with Agile processes, all members have equal rights and help each other wherever and whenever there is need. Employees are not on their own.

**May make mistakes:** Even if you don't ask the team members to make mistakes, you can at least take away their fear of mistakes. In Agile, a mistake is something the team can learn from and is therefore not taken personally.

**Clear work:** In an Agile project, employees always have the whole picture in mind, not just the parts they are working on. They have a better understanding of the project and can also estimate how big their share is.

**Get work yourself:** In most Agile projects, employees can take on the work they think they can do best. This is also done in consultation with the team, but the individual members are better able to contribute themselves and their qualifications than in classic waterfall projects where the work is often assigned not according to abilities but according to who is currently free.

You can also help yourself with a table that shows quite clearly which hurdles have to be overcome. In every company there is the behavior that you believe that what you do is not only right but also the only and best way. It also clearly shows the difference between the industrial age, which was mainly characterized by production, and the modern, complex computer age, which is based on services.

| Beliefs in the Industrial Age | Beliefs in the Computer Age |
|---|---|
| We can plan the work and work according to plan. | Planning is important, plans are unimportant. |
| The three elements volume, budget and time can be exchanged against each other to solve problems. | Time and budget are constants, only the extent of the work can be changed. |
| A plan gets better and better over time as we move into the requirements, design, development, testing and delivery phases. | A plan gets better and better over time because it is constantly reviewed and adapted to the team and its performance. |
| You can always try to solve problems later with a change request. | The scope is flexible and change requests are always welcome. |
| My job is to supervise the plan. | I can't control a plan. Handing the team over to the arms of Agile is my only chance to control something. So I coach the |

|  | team to make them more Agile. |
|---|---|
| Completing tasks and reaching milestones demonstrates the progress of the project. | Only finished products demonstrate how far a project has come. |

*Table from* "Coaching Agile Teams" *from Lyssa Adkins, 2010, Addison-Wesley.*

You will usually be called in as a coach for two reasons: Either to support teams and individuals as a kind of mentor in introducing Agile methods or to help them implement them. In football, for example, this is like the difference between explaining the strategy and training on the pitch.

The above arguments are quite good for preparing a team for the changes that will come with Scrum and other methods.

 **But as an Agile Coach you will also have to show the team how to really put this into practice.**

If such coaching is your task, then here again the urgent advice that you should be really competent in it applies. A soccer coach who can't shoot a proper free kick and can't even dribble a little is not taken seriously. It's always better if you've worked on Scrum or Kanban projects yourself and maybe even been a Product Owner or Scrum Master before taking on a coaching job.

# 7.3 Coaching Sessions

Most of the time, the coaching is held in **coaching sessions,** to which the team is called. The problem is often that this is another meeting that keeps employees from their actual tasks. It has become common practice to reduce these meetings to a minimum, especially since there are already many meetings at Scrum. Informal meetings, called **Brown Bag** sessions in the US, have proven to be more effective. Employees usually bring their lunch—often a sandwich or a burger—in a brown paper bag, and people talk about problems with the project during the lunch break. However, this doesn't work in every company; especially where lunch breaks are sacred, you should consider this type of conversation carefully. And of course you shouldn't overdo it and steal the team's lunch break permanently. But the Brown Bag sessions are always effective when there are acute things to discuss.

As an example we would like to show you how you can bring in the topic of sprint goals. For this you will need a meeting room and if possible a whiteboard or a flipchart. Özmen Adibelli works as an Agile Coach at ACM, a software company. He described in a blog post[6] how he tried to explain sprint goals to the team less as a teacher but rather as a facilitator. Open questions can help.

**What are we doing here?**

After you have welcomed the workshop participants, you ask why they all came together today. Most will not have expected the question and know that the answer "because we are doing a workshop" is not really what you want. But it's not about the right answer, it's about making it clear that active participation is desired. Your workshop is not a place to sit back and read Facebook messages under the table. To make this clear, it is better to involve the participants right from the start. Özmen Adibelli then gives the initial basic information about the Sprint Goal and how to learn to formulate and achieve these goals. Another question he likes to ask is how often Sprint Goals are mentioned in the Scrum Guide. Some will call the number

---

[6] Adibelle, Ö.: How to Facilitate a Scrum Sprint Goal Session (2018). URL: http://www.scrumexpert.com/knowledge/ how-to-facilitate-a-scrum-sprint-goal-session/ [Date of Reference: 25-08-2018]

zero, others between five and ten. The correct answer is 26. Again, it is not about who really knows this number. It's about showing how important Scrum Goals are. These little exercises serve to break the ice and let everyone speak once. Usually it is easier to speak again if you have already done so once.

 **As a moderator each workshop is something special for you, you have prepared yourself for it, you accept the challenge and you are curious who the participants are. Your excitement does not necessarily have to be shared by the participants. For them, the workshop is usually mandatory, keeps them from their regular work, and for some it's just another meeting on a long list of meetings.**

**What and Why**

Of course, a coach cannot avoid imparting some basic knowledge during a workshop on sprint goals. As professionals in this field, we often tend to think we have to explain all aspects down to the smallest detail and the participants are always eager to learn. Unfortunately, the reality is somewhat different. Listening is a very bad way to learn. A teacher at school therefore has a blackboard: to visualize things, even if they are only words. We can remember pictorial elements more easily. In the case of the Sprint Goals workshop, Özmen Adibelli mostly uses small mind maps. These have the advantage that you can develop them slowly, but everyone involved always has an overview. They also help you as a coach to see where you are right now. You can therefore jump back and forth more easily.

**Own Experiences**

Most participants will have come into contact with sprint goals before, and now is a good opportunity to ask them about them.

- What experiences have they had?
- What was good?
- What wasn't so good?

It's more about short answers and not everyone has to answer these questions. The answers given can be helpful later, so you should write them in keywords on the whiteboard or flipchart.

**How?**

Once you've covered the What and Why topic, it's time to start looking at the How. Your participants will now be able to interact with you as well as with each other. Now you ask them how they formulate a sprint goal. You write down their suggestions on the blackboard. This involves the participants, keeps them awake and they feel that their participation has value.

As a workshop leader you will experience surprises again and again. You will see that active participants notice things you would never have thought of. Therefore, it is important that you are able to adapt to them again and again. Özmen Adibelli tells from his practice:

> "I had 'what if cases' planned in a certain part of the workshop. But people didn't want to wait until they got to that point. They already asked that in the 'how' part. So I just took both parts together. But I made sure that it was clear which example was related to which part. So we could discuss how, what and why together without watering it down."

## What if?

Questions that are asked of you often tempt you to give a direct answer. After all, you are the expert and you know the answer. But that doesn't always help the team. You should have two things in mind before you give the right answer:

**1**. You don't always know the purpose behind a question. So first try to summarize the question and ask if you have understood it correctly.

**2.** Ask the other members what answer they would give. There is not always only one correct answer and often valuable discussions and exchanges arise that would not have taken place with a quick answer from you in this form.

Özmen Adibelli's advice to a coach: "Even if you have your own ideas, remember that others have different approaches and everyone learns differently. Remember the old saying, 'Nothing I say is necessarily right or wrong.' Therefore try to get the participants to participate as much as possible, be happy about the feedback and be able to change something at any time.

# 7.4 How Best to Ask as a Coach

It is a truism that one should avoid closed questions—those that can be answered with yes or no—if one wants to get a meaningful answer, and yet we still find ourselves asking such questions over and over again. As a coach, you will need to pay special attention to how questions are asked to employees. Here are a few examples:

| | | |
|---|---|---|
| Are the priorities in the product catalogue well arranged? | → | What would you change about the order? |
| Have you got enough work in the sprints? | → | What free capacities do you still have? |
| Did the team understand Scrum as a method? | → | What else needs to be explained? |
| Are all team members satisfied with their roles? | → | Which roles need to be changed? |

Something a coach should also avoid is asking the team or individual members why. You have to ask yourself this question, but in the team it can be perceived as pressure or criticism. For example, if a sprint was not canceled after the agreed time, you should not ask the staff why they did it. On the one hand they certainly didn't do it out of bad faith or for fun, on the other hand you want to find out if there is a problem in the workflow. So it would be better to ask if it was a one-time incident, because you wanted to finish something, or if it is a systemic problem and can happen often (for example, because subsequent processes are only set in motion after completion, which would not happen if work only goes back to the product backlog). Questions that you can formulate with "How can you..." or "What can you do that..." give the team the opportunity to think about a solution or to analyze the problem.

You have another task at meetings when it comes to having discussions. Even if you have the best agenda and a meeting is time boxed, it can happen again and again that a discussion gets out of hand.

 **Two types of behavior are most common: Someone talks for too long and someone attacks another person personally.**

It is actually considered rude to interrupt someone, but sometimes you have no other choice. Instead of just running over the other person, you can try to start the interruption with a short summary of what the person has said so far. This often takes the wind out of their sails. Another method is to set time limits from the outset and to back this up with an acoustic signal.

If a discussion gets hot and employees start accusing and insulting each other, you have to intervene immediately and end the session. This is not about rebuking others but about taking the steam out and calming down. You can resume the meeting an hour later or at a later time. It's up to you and the team to decide whether to address what happened, but even then it should be discussed together: "How can we avoid attacking others personally?" Sometimes you can see tensions coming up like a thunderstorm.

 **What can help in such a case is movement. Take the team and go for a walk together to discuss everything. Movement helps to break down energy and can often nip emerging conflicts in the bud.**

Another method is **non-violent communication**. It was developed by Marshall Rosenberg and is based on four elements that are often present in a conflict-laden discussion and that one should be aware of. **Observation, feeling, need, desire.**

*An example is: "At the morning meetings you always come too late (observation). Somehow we don't seem to be important to you (feeling), but we only have 15 minutes (need). Can't you make it at least once on time (desire)?"*

You confront the other person with this and put him in a defensive position, which makes the spiral of conflict turn. If you now take these four points away from you and transfer them to the other person instead, by trying to understand the reason for your behavior, then it looks quite different.

*"I have seen that you often come late, and have the feeling that you are completely rushed. Should we postpone the meeting or how can we help you?"*

By empathically enriching the questions, we take out the conflict. You can use this technique for many other conflicts in a team. It is suitable not only for communication between two people but also in groups. "I have seen our Burndown Chart go up. If something burdens you, what is it? We can certainly solve it together. Do you want to try that?"

# 7.5 Systems Thinking

One method that cannot be learned overnight, but which you can understand quite quickly in principle, is Systems Thinking. In summary, it can be called an understanding that things and processes are interconnected at many different levels and act as a system. To break them down into individual components does not help to understand the system. Rather, one has to try to understand the relationships between the processes and also to accept that systems can grow together and thus produce new systems.

 **For you as a coach this means that a project is more than the sum of the team members and the method used.**

It is a system in which you are as embedded as anyone else, albeit with other connections. In order to test the system, it is not disassembled but tested following the Agile Philosophy, which changes of parameters cause which changes in the system. In more concrete terms, this means that the feedback loops that you already know from Scrum and testing can also be used in coaching. Understand the team as a system and always try to make changes in the team and observe the consequences together. Systems Thinking is above all a matter of attitude in which you accept that the world is not linear but complex and networked.

# 7.6 Coaching as a Facilitator

In his blog at Scrum.org Punit Doshi[7] describes the tasks of a coach in a team as follows:

 **"Make sure everyone on the team understands what it's all about. You will have to explain right at the start what the context is of the project and why you want to use Agile now. It may well be that you have to remind yourself of this over the course of the project."**

You'll have to make some rules that everyone involved has to accept. These rules relate mainly to when you start work in the morning and when you stop, whether it's allowed to use your phone, that meetings are mandatory, and what are the core values that Scrum stands for. You should also explain how conflicts can be resolved and what procedures exist.

**Make sure you're the only one talking.** What you want is for meeting participants and the team to communicate with each other. If everyone is silent, consider what might be the reason.

---

[7] Doshi, P. (2018): Agile Coach Toolkit #4: Effective Facilitation. URL: https://www.scrum.org/resources/blog/agile-coach-toolkit-4-effective-facilitation [Date of Reference: 24-07-2018]

**Create an atmosphere in which anyone can raise a problem and draw attention to a mistake** without pointing the finger at the culprit. Try to stop any personal attack immediately.

**Time constraints** for meetings often work wonders. Try to set a tight time limit for all meetings.

**Try to include those who are calmer in discussions**. You don't just want to let the champions talk, you want everyone to get involved.

An important task will be to feel the **mood in the team** and to intervene quickly if you notice that the energy changes into the negative.

**Always stay neutral**. You are committed to the project and not to the people. It's not about who's right, it's about how best to solve a problem so that everyone can continue working as quickly as possible.

The above points also apply to the work of the Scrum Master. In fact, the boundaries between a coach and a Scrum Master are blurred when it comes to a single team, and sometimes it is actually one and the same person. The Scrum Master has a somewhat narrower description, essentially that he is responsible for monitoring the Scrum rules. For teams without a coach, however, he will also take over the leadership of the team when it comes to solving general problems.

As a coach you will also be hired to train several teams. You will have to deal with Scrum Masters and Product Owners who need help to introduce or improve Scrum or other Agile techniques. The above tips also apply, but they will have to be implemented by the team leaders.

Especially when an Agile project is to be rolled out for several teams, it will be up to you to coordinate them. The above rules, for example, should apply to all teams. Everyone should have the same working hours. Nowadays, since some teams are scattered around the globe, you will also have to think together with the team leaders about how to coordinate work in  different time zones.

# 7.7 Coaching across Time Zones

Time zones are something that even the best technology cannot solve. In software development in particular, it is common today for teams to work across many countries and continents. When you wake up in Europe, you go to sleep in the USA and the Asians have their lunch break. If your company doesn't have the money to fly you to the respective teams, you will have no choice but to hold video conferences. It's always better to find the lowest common denominator when it comes to time.

 **Try to accommodate as many time zones as possible without having to get up at 4 a.m. or sit in the office at 11 p.m.**

The weekend, especially Sunday, should be taboo. With global teams you should also consider religious and cultural differences. Many Muslims go to Friday prayer, while Jews do not work on the Sabbath. That's why it's important to discuss conference dates with the team first, not just to see if they fit into your calendar.

It will happen again and again that not everyone can be on board. In this case you should try to **record the video conference** and make it available as a video for those who could not attend. Ideally, the video will also be published with a comment function so that those who were not there can ask questions afterwards. You should only use these videos with global teams. In a local team, participation is mandatory. If you are ill or have a client appointment, the content of the meeting will have to be explained by the other participants.

# 7.8 Solving Conflicts and Dealing with Stress

In a team that develops software, but also in entire organizations, conflicts inevitably arise, especially when working under pressure.

A Gallup study found that 80 percent of employees experience stress at work. Almost half of the workers said they needed some form of stress management. A follow-up study showed that 35 percent of employees felt that their work was affecting their health, and 42 percent said that work pressure was negatively affecting their private relationships.

According to the American Psychological Association, one third of all American employees suffer from a chronic form of stress. Similar observations have also been made by the

Federal Office for Occupational Safety and Health in a large-scale study. "In the majority of cases, there were consistent correlations between work condition factors and mental health, allowing work demands to be classified into stressors and resources."[8]

The fact that you have a lot of personal responsibility in an Agile project does not mean that there is no pressure and no stress. It only has other causes. Agile Coaches are increasingly being asked to solve conflicts. You can already read it in job advertisements. But that doesn't mean that an Agile project automatically causes problems. Rather, it shows that one is aware of the problems and wants to solve them. It's a bug that you have found, and it needs to be fixed. Here you come into play as a coach.

Pressure in the team can be caused by the following factors:

- When sprints come to an end but the work is not done
- Too many tests fail

---

[8] Bundesanstalt für Arbeitsschutz und Arbeitsmedizin: Psychische Gesundheit in der Arbeitswelt – Wissenschaftliche Standortbestimmung. URL: https://www.baua.de/DE/Angebote/Publikationen/Berichte/Psychische-Gesundheit.html [Date of Reference: 12-08-2018]

- The work in a Kanban project does not flow properly

- The burndown's wearing off

- The end of the project is approaching

- There are too many change requests

In addition, there are of course also many interpersonal problems that can occur within a team. There are know-it-alls who want to do everything themselves. There is one super-expert who shows off his expertise more than clearly. A Product Owner acts like a boss. A Scrum Master is overtaxed and doesn't want to admit that to himself. Stakeholders are constantly intervening.

As an Agile Coach you will sometimes feel like you are in a kindergarten and have to calm your mind, and sometimes you also have to put your foot down. But most of the time it is your job to help the team solve their conflicts on their own.

There are hundreds of conflict resolution methods, and you have probably already completed one or two workshops on this topic. But because it is an important part of the work of an Agile Coach, here again there is a small selection of different approaches.

## Conflict Cards

A short workshop with a conflict map can help, especially if there are always minor conflicts in a team that add up over time. In principle, this is a mind map, which is best applied to a large piece of paper. At the beginning the members can **write and attach conflicts on sticky notes**. Then they look together to see which conflicts may belong together or have the same or similar causes.

But it can also be used to solve a certain problem. It is written in the mind map in the middle; then the team tries to write down what you want and what you don't want. In the next step, different **solutions can be worked out**. You will take on the role of moderator and make sure that the discussion is focused and does not get out of hand.

## Naikan

Naikan is a Japanese concept of self-knowledge. It actually refers to one's own life story and one's relationship with other people but can also be very helpful in a group conflict by changing one's perspective. Dieter Rösner[9] is an expert in this field and has also spoken about it in a

---

[9] Rösner, D. (2018): Konfliktmanagement – für Scrum-Teams ein Muss! (3). URL: https://www.gudrun-kreisl.de/blog/eintrag/konfliktmanagement-fuer-scrum-teams-ein-muss-3/ [Date of Reference: 10-08-2018]

contribution. Instead of formulating what one wants, the point of view is reversed and one asks oneself the following questions:

- What did the team give me?

- What did I give the team?

- How did I interrupt the team?

The Agile Coach can turn it into a session that doesn't even have to last long. All team members present are first asked to answer these three questions in writing. It is important that calm prevails. You should not do this exercise in the canteen. It is good, for example, if there is a park where you can sit, preferably directly on the lawn.

When everyone has written down their answers, they form into pairs and the answers are exchanged in each pair. If the team consists of fewer than six people, the answers can also be communicated in a large circle. Such a round can last from 10 to 15 minutes. In the next step, the observations of the pairs can also be exchanged in a large circle. This should be rather short and concise. The point is not so much that everyone should remember what the other has said but that one should learn how the others are doing.

# 7.9 Stress in the Project: What to Do?

Again and again stressful situations will occur, which can easily escalate. Your skills as a mediator are particularly in demand here. As with conflict resolution, Agile Trainers have various tools to help the team with stress. Most of the time, the stress is caused by some doing their work faster and others taking longer. This means that one part of the team has to wait while another part feels a lot of pressure.

Try to show the team that there are differences in experience and skills between the members. Some have been doing a certain job for a long time, for others it's new territory. If you have more experience, you will usually be faster and faster.

 **Try to always refer to the team members and not to yourself.**

Avoid sentences like, "I need a day for a job like this, but you're gonna need two days." That just demotivates. The same applies within the team: Explain to the team members that they should not and must not compare themselves with others. The focus is on the team, not the individual members. Work can simply be distributed differently.

Everyone is expected to give their best but not to be better than others. One cause of stress and pressure can also be the Agile system itself because a team has to make promises every day and keep them. It starts with the Daily Stand Up and ends the moment you have referred to a job as Done. If a team couldn't finish a sprint, it can make you feel guilty. You feel responsible and afraid of making mistakes. This is the case with us humans and has nothing to do with Agile.

We don't feel good when we can't keep a promise. Often it is a question of the choice of words that can help. Team members don't have to promise to do anything, they just have to say that they are doing the job. That doesn't mean they won't give everything to finish the job. There should be so much honesty in an Agile team that no one deliberately tries to put the team at risk.

When individual team members experience stress, you can talk to them about those exact words. Ask them:

- How do you describe your work?

- What pressure do you feel?

- What expectations do you think are placed on you?

- Do you feel time pressure?

The latter is above all a problem for teams that have previously worked with a classic project management system. Here the members are driven from one milestone to the next, and due dates hover above everyone like the Sword of Damocles. At Agile, you'll have to tell the team that time is not the most important factor. If someone can't finish the work today, he or she still has time tomorrow. It's more important that the work is done well.

Also ask in the team if they have set a **certain number of hours for certain tasks**. Actually this should not be the case, but some companies let their employees write down the hours in order to be able to bill better or easier afterwards. However, this contradicts the Agile idea. That's why you should always talk about the fact that hourly targets increase pressure and stress but don't improve the product. The only time unit at Scrum, for example, is the sprint.

Of course, you will have to estimate how much time and resources a project will need for it to be completed, also to determine what will be done in the sprints. But here you can suggest a trick to the team: Instead of thinking in hours or in man hours, they should divide the tasks into three or four categories: Very difficult, difficult, medium, and easy. This makes it easier for the employees to estimate the effort and at the same time you feel better: If a task is not finished, that's okay because it's difficult. At the same time it motivates when difficult tasks are solved faster than expected.

In a blog post for Admag, Mark Balbes[10] described what inner stress can look like that accumulates at some point and can really slow down a team.

 **Put yourself in the position of a programmer.**

In an Agile environment, programmers have a lot of personal responsibility and are allowed to divide up large parts of the work themselves. Balbes describes how a programmer has already thought about what he wants to do today and would like to get started. But then he has to wait for the morning meeting, and because today new pairs are formed for programming, he is assigned a new task in which he is not really an expert. But pair

---

[10] Balbes, M.: The Stress of Agile (2017). URL:
https://adtmag.com/articles/2017/01/24/stress-of-agile.aspx
[Date of Reference: 14-08-2018]

programming also serves to distribute knowledge and to ensure that teams don't just consist of pure experts. Finally, the Agile Coach also gives the task to write down how often a couple discusses and how much of it is task related. Your couple partner is an expert in what needs to be done and fears that a deadline will have to be met. He therefore hardly lets you touch the keyboard. Then the pairs are exchanged again, but you are the one who keeps the story and must now explain something to another person that was not explained to you before.

Often Agile Coaches don't see what's happening inside a programmer and developer and how the well-intentioned methods are actually recorded. Openness and learning together can also often cause stress when team members can't finish other things. That's why you should always ask for feedback as to whether, for example, pair programming really helps the team or whether the differences in knowledge and skills are too big.

The feedback of the individual team members is very important for the Agile Coach. However, you will also have to make sure that these feedbacks do not lead to new tasks that could cause stress. It is simply best to observe the team and if you feel that someone is less busy at the moment, take the opportunity to ask how the person is doing and how they feel.

**Yoga**

Sometimes a coach has to think outside his normal way of working. Stress can't always be solved only with conversations or a changed workflow. If you are under pressure and tense, you need to learn to relax, and one possible way might be yoga. You don't really have to retrain as a yoga teacher. It is enough if you know some basic exercises that you can do at work without a yoga mat.

There are many good reasons for practicing yoga at work:

- Employees who are happy and full of energy are more productive

- There are fewer sickness notifications caused by stress

- Employees can concentrate better

- Employees can react more calmly and evenly in stressful situations

- Tensions in the head, neck and shoulders are reduced, as are pain in the forearm, insomnia, high blood pressure and problems caused by working on a keyboard

Healthy and balanced employees are also friendlier and better at customer service, have better team behavior and are less likely to quit a job. Employees suffer less from burnout, which is positively reflected in the burndown chart. Studies also show that yoga and other relaxation techniques can reduce aggression in the workplace. Finally, employees have less physical pressure from tension, which also has a positive effect on overall well-being. They literally come to work less tense.

Which exercises are possible? If you really want to introduce yoga into a team for a long time (and this should be understood preventively, i.e. before stress occurs), then you should consult a yoga teacher who will at least advise you during the first few hours as a coach and help you perform the exercises. If, on the other hand, you want to try out how the topic is received by the staff, here are a few very simple yoga positions from Career Bible.[11]

> **Turn your head:** Slowly tilt the head forward until the chin almost touches the chest. Then slowly turn the head to the left as well. Repeat this exercise several times and also turn the head to the right.

---

[11] Warkentin, N.: Yoga-Übungen: Tipps für Anfänger (und fürs Büro). URL: https://karrierebibel.de/yoga-uebungen/ [Date of Reference: 28-08-2018]

**Stretch back**: Stand with both feet on the floor, bend slightly forward and place palms on knees. Then stretch your back and look up with your head— inhale. Now roll up your back a little, look at the floor and exhale. Repeat the exercise five times.

**Stretch your arms:** Sit straight on a chair, cross your hands behind your back and stretch out upwards. Hold this position for a few seconds. Then lower your arms (still crossed) and lower your upper body slightly towards your thighs, stretching your neck slightly.

# 8. Let the Project Run

The third phase of Agile coaching is the most difficult for many trainers. They need to learn to retreat now. It is often referred to as passive coaching, even if it is somewhat misleading because you will not really just watch the team at work. But your task will change from an active trainer to a manager. Just as in football the manager no longer leads the training sessions himself, you will also be more concerned with the strategy and progress of the project and only intervene when help is needed.

## 8.1 Improve the Team

You can improve the team at any time by—if you are allowed to—making personnel and spatial changes. A coach should and may think and act holistically.

**Try to create a safe space**

Google once asked its employees[12] what they thought was the most important reason for a successful team. The

---

[12] Sheffield, H. (2016): Google spends years figuring out that the to a good working environment is just to be nice – Successful teams have a high "average social sensitivity". URL: https://www.independent.co.uk/news/business/news/google-workplace-wellbeing-perks-benefits-human-behavioural-

answers were surprising: successful teams weren't those that were staffed by the best of the best; they were those who were offered a psychologically safe space because then the members could work best.

We work faster, more concentrated and more effectively if we don't have to be afraid, if we are able to make suggestions, if we can also criticize the work of others. Exchange and constructive criticism are particularly important in an Agile environment. Such a corporate culture and safe spaces are not built overnight but they pay off.

**Hire people who are capable and fit into the company**
If it is also your job as a coach to put the team together; then you will have to make sure that the members also fit into an Agile environment. You don't just need specialists sitting alone in front of your computer, you need people who can work closely with others and who are able to take criticism. Nevertheless, you should also pay attention to their abilities. It is not so much a question of whether someone is competent in a certain computer language but rather what a person can bring along to further develop the team.

---

psychology-safety-a6917296.html [Date of Reference: 01-08-2018]

## Development comes first

Don't curse yourself. Even if you first have to learn who is in your team and how a company is structured, you should get to work as quickly as possible and get the team into production. Each team is different, and you will most likely learn what is different when you see how they work. Developers should be interviewed as early as possible, even at the planning stage of the project.

 **As a coach you should not only think about the actual execution but also about what happens before.**

So let your developers play around and develop ideas as early as possible. Later on, this will also pay off in terms of higher motivation because they feel that they are being taken seriously.

## Bring your team together

Even though it's chic today to have your developers scattered all over the world, and it can be pleasant for a programmer to work from the beach in Asia, it's always better to have the team physically together. This solves time zone problems as well as cooperation problems. Especially in a company that uses Xtreme Programming, it is indispensable that you literally sit together. Virtual collaboration can work, but it always comes with big challenges. If you have the resources, bring your team together physically. If you only communicate with others via Slack, you don't really know people. Important elements of communication such as tone of voice or gestures and facial expressions, external appearance and even smells are completely lost.

**Get everyone together**

A team will be able to work better if it is not isolated. You should always try to involve the other stakeholders in meetings. If you work as a coach with several teams, try to create occasions where they can exchange ideas and get to know each other. With Agile projects it is always better to know what the big picture looks like. Especially in a German team, what you like to say about Germans is true: "Germans always want to have an overall concept."[13] The more you understand the connections, the better you can make the product.

---

[13] Ciprian, B. / Secara-Onita, A.: The peculiarities of German negotiation style. URL:
http://steconomiceuoradea.ro/anale/volume/2013/n2/002.pdf
[Date of Reference: 04-08-2018]

## 8.2 How and When to Retire as a Coach

The process of withdrawal can take several days or even weeks. There is rarely a deadline when you suddenly stop coming to the office and let yourself be seen only once a week. Rather, you will gradually reduce your attendance. But when is the best time to start?

Ultimately, every coach will have to decide for himself, but there are some indications that you can slowly leave the team to its own devices. One is that the daily standups run smoothly and on time. Another is good development of the Burndown Charts, which means that the work will be done within the estimated time. The team has learned to organize itself and at Scrum the Scrum Master has taken the initiative and knows how to support the team. With a Kanban system, it is a good indicator if the work flows evenly and the columns are always evenly filled but not too much work is parked.

 **It depends a little on the contract in which your coaching is regulated how long such a transition phase lasts. Depending on the size of the project, it can take several months.**

# 8.3 When to Intervene

Sabine Canditt and Dr. Peter Braun have described in an article about Scrum and the Agile Method one of the traps that many a trainer and Scrum Master could fall into:

> "After initial successes with Scrum, it often comes to a disillusionment. Obstacles become clearly visible, which cannot be solved by individuals or teams quickly in passing, e.g. the lack of correct and important information, unclear and lengthy decision paths or inefficient tool support. It is a big advantage of Scrum that these problems become clear - and yet the organization is often not prepared for them. Absurdly, it is not the recognition of the problem that is booked to the Scrum account, but the cause of the problem. The Agile coach is not limited to finding simplified ad hoc solutions that often aggravate the problem rather than improve it. Instead, he supports the problem analysis by clarifying complex interrelationships that often only take effect with a certain delay[14]."

---

[14] Canditt, S. / Dr. Braun, P.: Scrum-Coaching: Hilfe zur Selbsthilfe. URL: https://www.sigs-datacom.de/uploads/tx_dmjournals/canditt_braun_OS_03_09.pdf [Date of Reference: 15-07-2018]

In the transition phase, your intervention is always appropriate if the team cannot solve the problem or if it has not yet recognized a problem. Your task during this time is to monitor the team's progress. The Burndown Charts are a measure but also are possible absences and dissatisfaction. For example, if many members of a team want to be assigned to another team, this is not a good sign. In this phase you will also have more to do with the Scrum Master and help him do his job and less work with the team itself.

# 9. Developing Yourself as a Coach

As a coach you will certainly not only want to develop your team but also yourself. After all, this is also the foundation of Agile development: permanent improvement, also of your own abilities. In their book, Rachel Davies and Liz Sedley suggest the following to keep you up to date:[15]

- Read one technical book per month

- Write your own blog

- Work on an Open Source project

- Write one post per day on a mailing list that deals with coaching

- Listen to weekly podcasts on technical topics and Agile

- Go to a meeting of Agile users once a month

You don't have to do everything written in this list, and if you're not living in a big city, you'll probably also have trouble finding weekly Agile meetings. It's all about staying mentally in motion, knowing what's happening in the

---

[15] Davies R. / Sedley, L.: Agile Coaching (2009), S. 208

scene and what new methods and approaches there are. One danger with coaching is that at some point you will reach a knowledge level because you are too busy coaching. But software development is a rapidly developing and changing field. It can quickly happen that you miss the boat and your new team looks at you in amazement because you don't know how it works.

# 9.1 Create Capacities for Your Own Coaches

If you are hired as a coach, many contracts state that you should also try to create the capacity for the organisation to produce its own coaches. Especially if you train several teams or even work at management level, you are confronted with the task of passing on your knowledge. This is part of life in an agile environment: knowledge is shared and others are enabled to expand their knowledge and acquire new skills. That's why it's so important that a coach has worked with Agile projects before and maybe even was a Scrum Master. The classic career in Agile is as follows:

**Programmer/Developer -> Product Owner -> Scrum Master -> Agile Coach -> Coach Trainer**

This does not mean that every developer has to become an Agile Coach. You can't just have chiefs, you also need Indians says old wisdom. Many programmers are more than happy with what they are doing and want to learn more in other areas, such as learning new programming languages and devoting themselves to a different technical topic. Others want to move to a more abstract level, and that's the Scrum Master and the coach.

In your team it is mostly the already mentioned champions who are best suited for the next step. Despite the best knowledge of human nature, you should better ask if someone really wants to develop in this direction.

While you are training a team, you will have little time to train individual members. Your focus will be on the Scrum Master(s) because they are well suited to coach other teams later because of their role. A football analogy also works here: Often the captain of a team also becomes a coach after his active career. Others get a job at the coaching academy.

You can either train new coaches in-house in workshops, or you can set up your own kind of academy and offer further training to become an Agile Coach.

## 9.2 Taking Coaching to a New Level

As a coach who has just started, you will surely train teams and support the Scrum Master. That's also why we have so many examples of this type of coaching. But at some point you will also want to improve yourself and not only help one team but coach several teams and their Scrum Masters in a company or even make the company and its management more Agile. Here it will no longer be about technical details like stand-up and sprints but about methods for how to plan less in management and how to care more about continuous improvement.

IT-Agile explains how and why Agile Leadership has to be trained differently than a team of software developers:

> "For effective agile leadership, both systemic issues (**system cycle**) must be clarified and relationships between individuals and teams strengthened (**trust cycle**).

"*The* **system cycle** *starts with* **working in agile teams**. *The agile work will uncover obstacles that cannot be solved locally in the teams (***Identify Impediments***). In the training, the participants learn techniques with which the obstacles can be analysed and solutions can be defined and tested by means of experiments. These solutions always strive towards a simplified organizational structure (***Reduce Org. Structure***). The relationships between the agile teams are also designed to be agile; agile teams do not yet make an* **agile organization**. *The agile teams must have* **agile relationships** *with each other. The simpler the organizational structure and the more agile the relationships between the teams, the more flexible and effective the agile teams can work. And so the system cycle begins again.*

"*A purely structural perspective runs the risk of only looking at structures and processes and neglecting the relationship level between people. The* **trust cycle** *therefore focuses on the relationships between those involved. The strengthening of trust (***Increase Trust***) is essential for this. In the training, the participants learn techniques to strengthen trust. On this basis, responsibility can grow (***Foster Responsibility***). More responsibility allows the reduction of the organizational structure (***Reduce Org. Structure***). A* *reduced organizational structure allows us to [...] require a greater degree of trust and the trust cycle goes into another round.*

*The **leadership cycle** is the driver of the system and trust cycles. Leadership becomes the more effective the clearer the purpose of the organization (**organizational purpose**) and the leader(s) (personal purpose) is. In the training, the participants get to know **leadership development models** with which the organizational as well as the personal purpose can be developed. Agile Leadership develops continuously. Feedback is the basis to check one's own leadership behaviour (**Get Feedback**) and to develop it further (**Develop Yourself**).*"[16]

Particularly if you want to develop into a coach for Agile Leadership, you should first gain experience in several projects with teams and then further your education. At IT Agile, for example, there are continuing education courses for Agile Coaches who want to take themselves to a new level.

---

[16] IT-agile: Führungskräfte-Ausbildung (Agile Leadership) - Inhalte der Ausbildung. URL: https://www.it-agile.de/ausbildung/fuehrungskraefte/ [Date of Reference: 18-07-2018]

**Coaching teams need both good knowledge of how to train and the necessary amount of experience.**

You shouldn't rush into anything and start your own academy right after your first job. In the Agile environment it is usual to include references anyway. The more you have, the more likely it is that a company will commission you with larger jobs.

If you want to assess yourself better, a small table compiled by Karen Greaves for Agile Coaches can help.[17] This table consists of horizontal columns divided into Coaching, Facilitation, Knowledge, Self and Training. The vertical column contains the terms Shu Ha and Ri, which come from the Japanese art of learning. They denote the different levels of basic knowledge, active practice and the ability to create something new on one's own.

---

[17] Greaves, K.: Assessiong Your Agile Coaching Skills (2018): URL: http://www.scrumexpert.com/knowledge/assessing-your-agile-coaching-skills/ [Stand:26-07-2018]

# 10. Summary

This book does not claim to train you as an Agile Coach. Rather, it should arouse your interest in the activity and give you some background knowledge. Even if you don't want to become a coach, you will have learned with the book how a coach thinks (or should think) and perhaps develop some understanding of his actions.

But if you really consider becoming an Agile Coach yourself, then hopefully you have more knowledge now than before. Coaching is above all an activity that requires many soft skills: The calmer and more balanced you are, the more you will be able to reassure a team. The more empathy you show, the more likely the employees are to open up emotionally. The more you are able to trust others, the easier it will be for you to let the team take responsibility for itself. In their book *Agile Coaching*, Rachel Davies and Liz Sedley have created a checklist for the Agile Coach that can help you decide whether you want to and can take on a project at all. Ask yourself the following questions and answer them in writing. Then have a cup of coffee, return after an hour and read the answers all over again.

**Motivation**

Why do I coach this team/company?

What do I want to change?

What do I want to learn from it?

**Own abilities**

What experience and knowledge can I offer?

What does the client need to know about me and my CV?

What does the team need to know about me?

**Responsibility**

Who are the stakeholders in the project?

What is my official role and are my tasks clearly defined?

Do these tasks conflict with Agile practices?

What measures do I have to measure my progress?

How do I know my task is done?

**Support**

Who in the company can support me? Who can be my mentor?

How will I be presented to the team?

Will I work with other coaches or Scrum Masters?

In most cases you will start as a coach of a Scrum team. The above mentioned book, *Agile Coaching*, is recommended, it is a standard work and deals in more detail with the tasks of a Scrum Coach. When it comes to coaching multiple teams, you can read the book *Coaching Agile Teams: A Companion for Scrum Masters, Agile Coaches* by Lyssa Adkins, which also provides a very detailed description of working with multiple teams.

You will have learned a lot in this book about how to motivate, understand and analyze teams. A good coach is characterized above all by his psychological abilities. Which techniques are used, whether you do yoga together, use Naikan or how to hold a Scrum-Meeting depends on whether there is a problem that needs to be solved. It is not your task to introduce Scrum unless you have been explicitly hired as a Scrum Master (in this case you should read a book about Scrum). Rather, you should help others to do their work better. You explain what Agile means and you are an expert in the methods, but your knowledge is only used when it is really needed by the team. And one last tip:

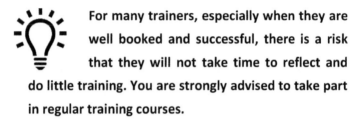 **For many trainers, especially when they are well booked and successful, there is a risk that they will not take time to reflect and do little training. You are strongly advised to take part in regular training courses.**

Good luck with your first coaching job!
Markus Heimrath

# Copyright and legal notice

This work including all its contents is protected by copyright. Reproduction, in whole or in part, as well as storage, processing, duplication and distribution by means of electronic systems, in whole or in part, is forbidden without the written permission of the Author. All translation Rights reserved.

The contents of this book were searched on the basis of recognized sources and examined with utmost care. However, the Author assumes no guarantee regarding the timeliness, accuracy and completeness of the information provided.

Liability claims against the author relating to the damages of any health, material or ideal nature caused by the use or non-use of the information provided for or by the use of incorrect and incomplete information are in principle excluded, so far, removed from the Author. Intentionally or grossly negligent. This book does not replace medical or professional advice and care.

This book refers to third-party content. The author expressly declares that at the time of creation of the link, no illegal content was identifiable on the pages to be linked. The Author has no influence on the related content. Therefore, the Author hereby explicitly distances himself from the content of all linked pages that have been modified after the link was set. For illegal, incorrect or incomplete content and in particular for damages resulting from the use or non-use of this information, the provider of the page in question, but not the Author of this book, is responsible.

Copyright Markus Heimrath
Edition 06/2019
No Section of the text may be used in any form without the consent of the Author.
Contact: Tim Ong/Türkstr. 4/30167 Hannover
Cover photo: Rawpixel.com/shutterstock.com
Formatting: Markus Heimrath

# Bibliography

Adibelle, Ö.: How to Facilitate a Scrum Sprint Goal Session (2018). URL: http://www.scrumexpert.com/knowledge/how-to-facilitate-a-scrum-sprint-goal-session/ [Date of Reference: 25-08-2018]

Agilemanifesto.org: Manifesto for Agile Software Development. URL: http://agilemanifesto.org/ [Stand: 14-07-2018]

Balbes, M.: The Stress of Agile (2017). URL: https://adtmag.com/articles/2017/01/24/stress-of-agile.aspx [Date of Reference: 14-08-2018]

Bundesanstalt für Arbeitsschutz und Arbeitsmedizin: Psychische Gesundheit in der Arbeitswelt – Wissenschaftliche Standortbestimmung. URL: https://www.baua.de/DE/Angebote/Publikationen/Bericht e/Psychische-Gesundheit.html [Date of Reference: 12-08-2018]

Canditt, S. / Dr. Braun, P.: Scrum-Coaching: Hilfe zur Selbsthilfe. URL: https://www.sigs-datacom.de/uploads/tx_dmjournals/canditt_braun_OS_03_09.pdf [Date of Reference: 15-07-2018]

Ciprian, B. / Secara-Onita, A.: The peculiarities of German negotiation style. URL: http://steconomiceuoradea.ro/anale/volume/2013/n2/00 2.pdf [Date of Reference: 04-08-2018]

Davies R. / Sedley, L.: Agile Coaching (2009)

Doshi, P. (2018): Agile Coach Toolkit #4: Effective Facilitation. URL: https://www.scrum.org/resources/blog/agile-coach-toolkit-4-effective-facilitation [Date of Reference: 24-07-2018]

Greaves, K.: Assessiong Your Agile Coaching Skills (2018): URL: http://www.scrumexpert.com/ knowledge/assessing-your-agile-coaching-skills/ [Date of Reference:26-07-2018]

IT-agile: Führungskräfte-Ausbildung (Agile Leadership) - Inhalte der Ausbildung. URL: https://www.it-agile.de/ausbildung/fuehrungskraefte/ [Date of Reference: 18-07-2018]

Koch, A. S.: Adopting an Agile Method (2006). URL: http://www.methodsandtools.com/archive/archive.php?id=41 [Date of Reference: 16-08-2018]

Lal Patary, C. (2017): Case Studies on Agile Transformation. URL: https://www.linkedin.com/ pulse/case-studies-agile-transformation-chandan-lal-patary/ [Date of Reference: 08--08-2018]

Rösner, D. (2018):  Konfliktmanagement – für Scrum-Teams ein Muss! (3). URL: https://www.gudrun-kreisl.de/blog/eintrag/konfliktmanagement-fuer-scrum-teams-ein-muss-3/ [Date of Reference: 10-08-2018]

Sheffield, H. (2016): Google spends years figuring out that the to a good working environment is just to be nice – Successful teams have a high "average social sensitivity". URL: https://www.independent.co.uk/news/business/news/google-workplace-wellbeing-perks-benefits-human-behavioural-psychology-safety-a6917296.html [Date of Reference: 01-08-2018]

Warkentin, N.: Yoga-Übungen: Tipps für Anfänger (und fürs Büro). URL: https://karrierebibel.de/yoga-uebungen/ [Date of Reference: 28-08-2018]

Lightning Source UK Ltd.
Milton Keynes UK
UKHW020639021222
413181UK00012B/1936